MW01268434

Inspirations JOURNAL

ISBN 978-1-60260-619-7

Published by Barbour Publishing, Inc., P.O. Box 719, Uhrichsville, Ohio 44683
www.barbourbooks.com

Our mission is to publish and distribute inspirational products offering exceptional value and biblical encouragement to the masses.

Printed in China.

Be faithful in little things,
for in them our strength lies.

Mother Teresa

Love is a great beautifier.

Louisa May Alcott

Date and Time: ____________________

Place: ____________________

Today, I was inspired by: ____________________

Other inspiring thoughts:

*The most wasted of all days
is one without laughter.*

E. E. Cummings

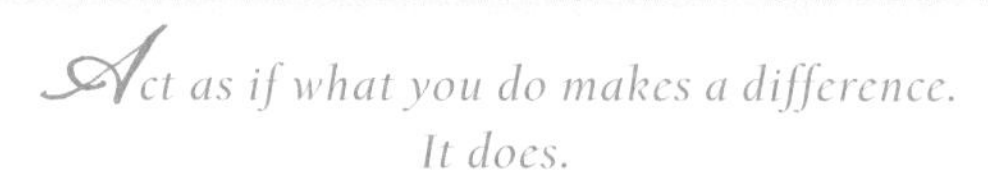
Act as if what you do makes a difference.
It does.

William James

Date and Time: ____________________

Place: ____________________

Today, I was inspired by: ____________________

Other inspiring thoughts:

You can trust the Lord too little,
but you can never trust Him too much.

Unknown

*This is the day which the LORD hath made;
we will rejoice and be glad in it.*

PSALM 118:24 KJV

Date and Time: ______________________

Place: ______________________

Today, I was inspired by: ______________________

Other inspiring thoughts:

Life is a splendid gift—
there is nothing small about it.

Florence Nightingale

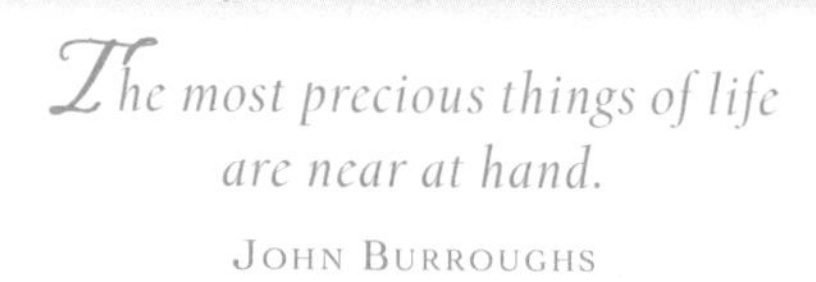

Date and Time: ______________________

Place: ______________________

Today, I was inspired by: ______________________

Other inspiring thoughts:

There's always something for which to be thankful.

Charles Dickens

To every thing there is a season,
and a time to every purpose under the heaven.

ECCLESIASTES 3:1 KJV

Date and Time: ______________________

Place: ______________________

Today, I was inspired by: ______________________

Other inspiring thoughts:

More things are wrought by prayer
than this world dreams of.

Alfred, Lord Tennyson

Fill up the crevices of time
with the things that matter most.

Amy Carmichael

Date and Time: ______

Place: ______

Today, I was inspired by: ______

Other inspiring thoughts:

The creation of a thousand forests is in one acorn.

Ralph Waldo Emerson

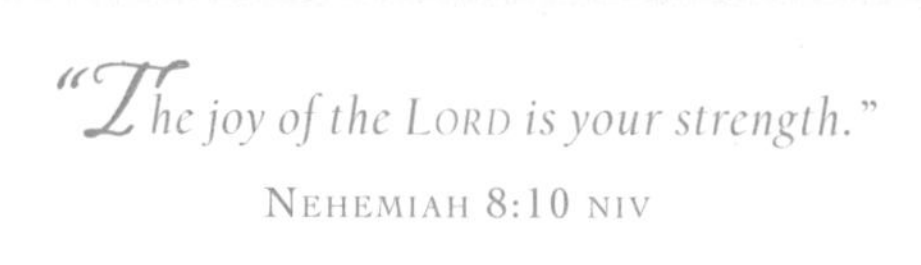

"The joy of the LORD is your strength."

NEHEMIAH 8:10 NIV

Date and Time: ______________________________

Place: ______________________________

Today, I was inspired by: ______________________________

Other inspiring thoughts:

Where the soul is full of peace and joy, outward surroundings and circumstances are of comparatively little account.

Hannah Whitall Smith

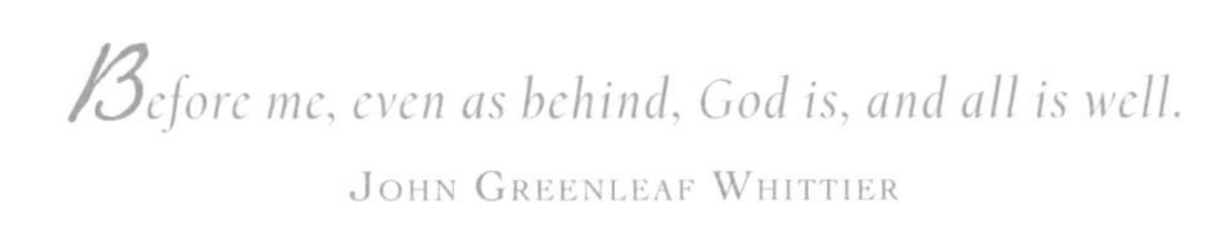

Date and Time: ______________________

Place: ______________________

Today, I was inspired by: ______________________

Other inspiring thoughts:

A gentle word, a kind look, a good-natured smile can work wonders and accomplish miracles.

William Hazlitt

Date and Time: ____________________

Place: ____________________

Today, I was inspired by: ____________________

Other inspiring thoughts:

In what seems ordinary and everyday there is always more than at first meets the eye.

Charles Cummings

When we do the best we can, we never know what miracle is wrought in our life, or in the life of another.

HELEN KELLER

Date and Time: ______

Place: ______

Today, I was inspired by: ______

Other inspiring thoughts:

Add to your joy by counting your blessings.

UNKNOWN

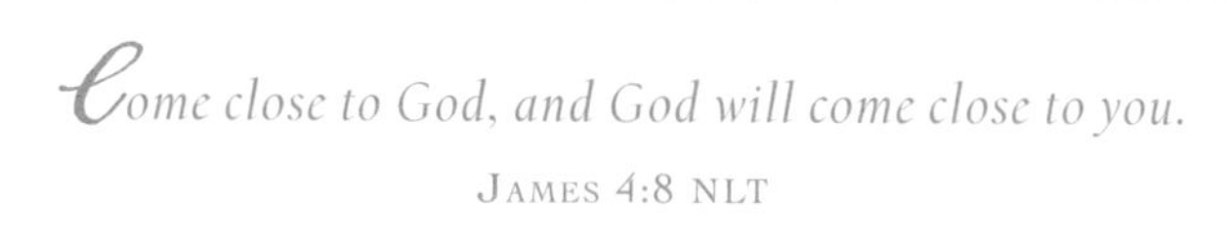

Come close to God, and God will come close to you.

James 4:8 NLT

Date and Time: ____________________

Place: ____________________

Today, I was inspired by: ____________________

Other inspiring thoughts:

The great doing of little things makes the great life.

EUGENIA PRICE

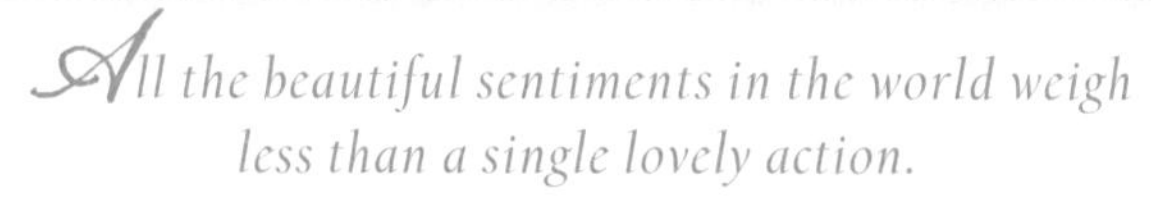

All the beautiful sentiments in the world weigh less than a single lovely action.

James Russell Lowell

Date and Time: __________

Place: __________

Today, I was inspired by: __________

Other inspiring thoughts:

We were not sent into this world to do anything into which we cannot put our hearts.

John Ruskin

*Pleasant words are as an honeycomb,
sweet to the soul, and health to the bones.*

PROVERBS 16:24 KJV

Date and Time: __________

Place: __________

Today, I was inspired by: __________

Other inspiring thoughts:

God loves each one of us as if there were only one of us.

Augustine

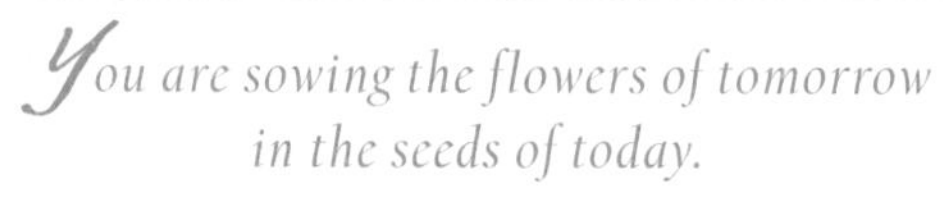

You are sowing the flowers of tomorrow
in the seeds of today.

UNKNOWN

Date and Time: ______________________

Place: ______________________

Today, I was inspired by: ______________________

Other inspiring thoughts:

What makes the desert so beautiful is that somewhere it hides a well.

Antoine de Saint-Exupéry

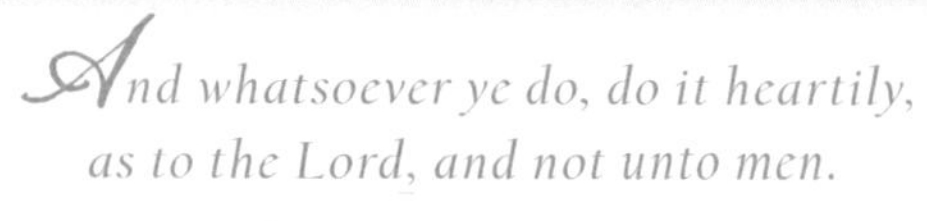

And whatsoever ye do, do it heartily,
as to the Lord, and not unto men.

COLOSSIANS 3:23 KJV

Date and Time: ______________________

Place: ______________________

Today, I was inspired by: ______________________

Other inspiring thoughts:

Resolve to see the world on the sunny side,
and you have almost won the battle of life at the outset.

SIR ROGER L'ESTRANGE

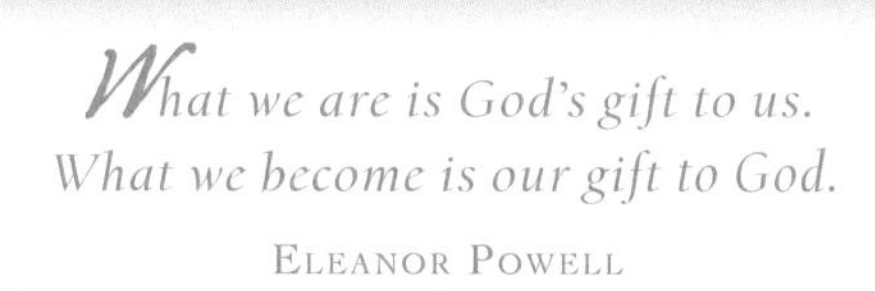

Date and Time: ______________________

Place: ______________________

Today, I was inspired by: ______________________

Other inspiring thoughts:

Use what talent you possess: The woods would be very silent if no birds sang except those that sang best.

Henry Van Dyke

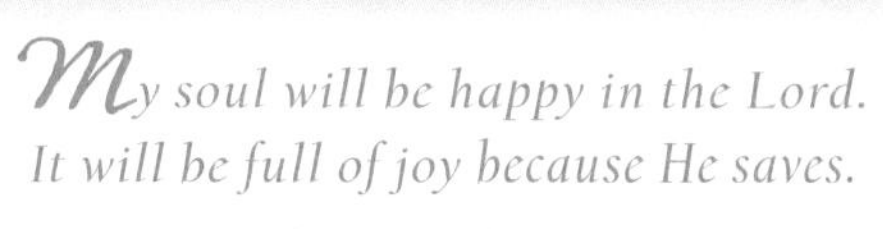

My soul will be happy in the Lord.
It will be full of joy because He saves.

Psalm 35:9 NLV

Date and Time: ______________________________

Place: ______________________________

Today, I was inspired by: ______________________________

Other inspiring thoughts:

Lovely flowers are the smiles of God's goodness.

William Wilberforce

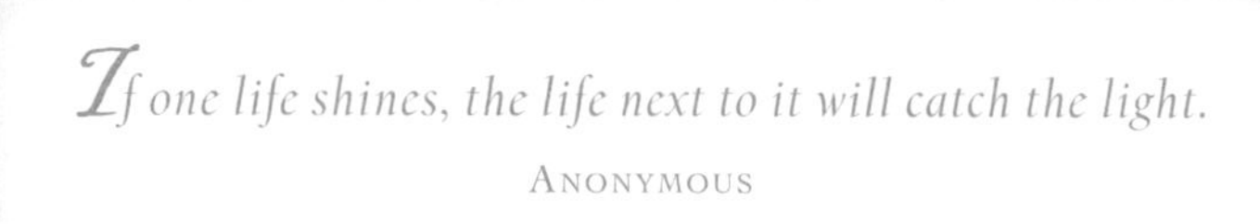

Date and Time: ______________________

Place: ______________________

Today, I was inspired by: ______________________

Other inspiring thoughts:

You are God's created beauty and the focus of His affection and delight.

Janet L. Weaver

Love never gives up, never loses faith, is always hopeful, and endures through every circumstance. . . . Love will last forever!

1 Corinthians 13:7–8 NLT

Date and Time: ______________________________

Place: ______________________________

Today, I was inspired by: ______________________________

Other inspiring thoughts:

Let there be many windows in your soul,
that all the glory of the universe may beautify it.

Ella Wheeler Wilcox

The joyful birds prolong the strain,
their songs with every spring renewed; the air we breathe,
and falling rain, each softly whispers: God is good.

John Hampden Gurney

Date and Time: ____________________

Place: ____________________

Today, I was inspired by: ____________________

Other inspiring thoughts:

Go confidently in the direction of your dreams!
Live the life you've imagined.

Henry David Thoreau

God is able to make all grace abound to you,
so that in all things at all times, having all that you need,
you will abound in every good work.

2 Corinthians 9:8 NIV

Date and Time: __________

Place: __________

Today, I was inspired by: __________

Other inspiring thoughts:

God's help is nearer than the door.

Irish Proverb

Pleasure is seldom found where it is sought. Our brightest blazes are commonly kindled by unexpected sparks.

Samuel Johnson

Date and Time: ______

Place: ______

Today, I was inspired by: ______

Other inspiring thoughts:

Everything has its wonders, even darkness and silence; and I learn, whatever state I am in, therein to be content.

Helen Keller

Every house is built by someone,
but God is the builder of everything.

HEBREWS 3:4 NIV

Date and Time: ______________________________

Place: ______________________________

Today, I was inspired by: ______________________________

Other inspiring thoughts:

The consciousness of loving and being loved brings a warmth and richness to life that nothing else can bring.

Oscar Wilde

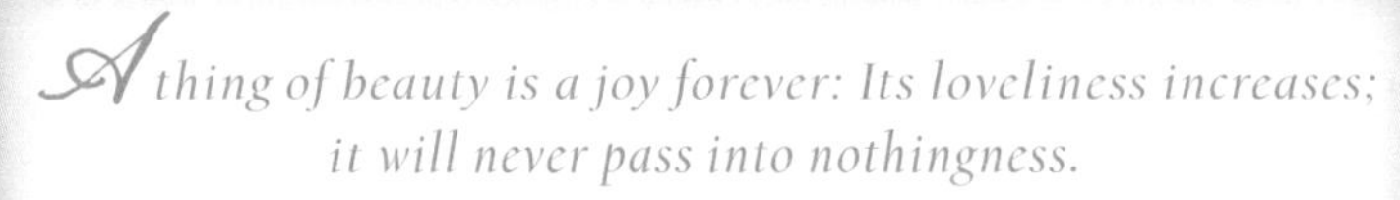

A thing of beauty is a joy forever: Its loveliness increases;
it will never pass into nothingness.

John Keats

Date and Time: ______________________

Place: ______________________

Today, I was inspired by: ______________________

Other inspiring thoughts:

God always gives the best to those who leave the choice with Him.

Unknown

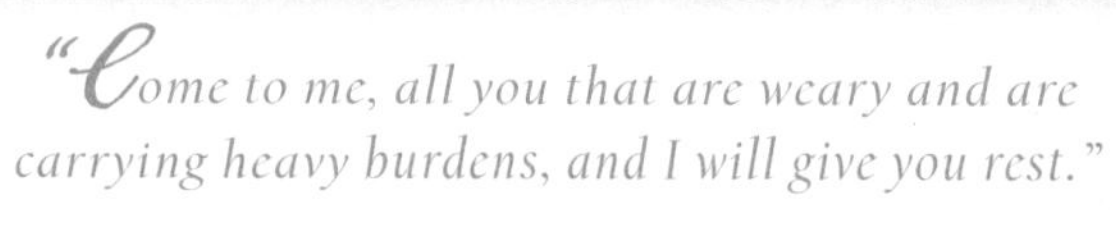

"Come to me, all you that are weary and are carrying heavy burdens, and I will give you rest."

Matthew 11:28 NRSV

Date and Time: ____________________

Place: ____________________

Today, I was inspired by: ____________________

Other inspiring thoughts:

Start by doing what's necessary, then what's possible, and suddenly you are doing the impossible.

Francis of Assisi

Life is what we are alive to. It is not length but breadth. . . . Be alive to. . .goodness, kindness, purity, love, history, poetry, music, flowers, stars, God, and eternal hope.

MALTBIE D. BABCOCK

Date and Time: ______

Place: ______

Today, I was inspired by: ______

Other inspiring thoughts:

Far away, there in the sunshine, are my highest aspirations. . . . I can look up and see their beauty, believe in them, and try to follow where they lead.

Louisa May Alcott

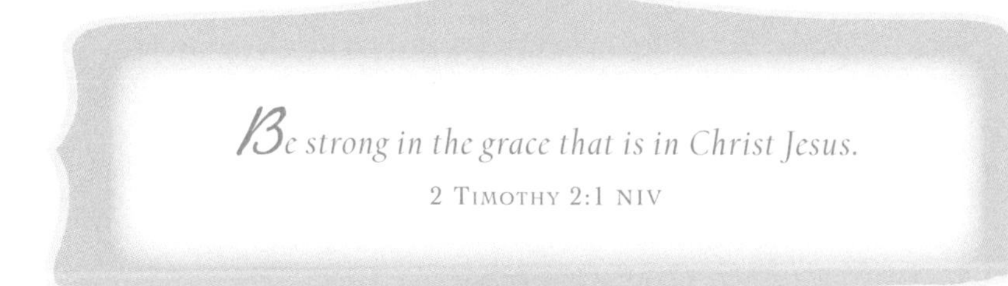

Date and Time: ______

Place: ______

Today, I was inspired by: ______

Other inspiring thoughts:

God's promises are like the stars;
the darker the night, the brighter they shine.

David Nicholas

There is no duty we so much underrate as the duty of being happy. By being happy we sow anonymous benefits upon the world.

ROBERT LOUIS STEVENSON

Date and Time:

Place:

Today, I was inspired by:

Other inspiring thoughts:

*Where others see but the dawn coming over the hill,
I see the soul of God shouting for joy.*

William Blake

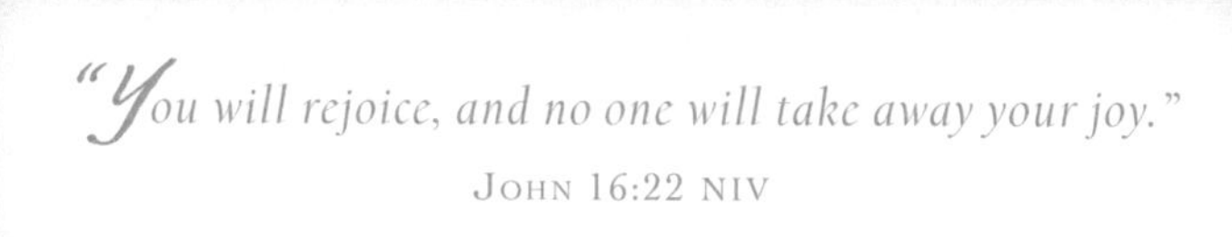

Date and Time: ______

Place: ______

Today, I was inspired by: ______

Other inspiring thoughts:

The splendor of the rose and the whiteness of the lily do not rob the little violet of its scent nor the daisy of its simple charm. If every tiny flower wanted to be a rose, spring would lose its loveliness.

Thérèse of Lisieux

We have a God who delights in impossibilities.

Andrew Murray

Date and Time: __________

Place: __________

Today, I was inspired by: __________

Other inspiring thoughts:

Sometimes our thoughts turn back toward a corner in a forest, or the end of a bank, or an orchard powdered with flowers, seen but a single time...[leaving] a feeling we have just rubbed elbows with happiness.

Guy de Maupassant

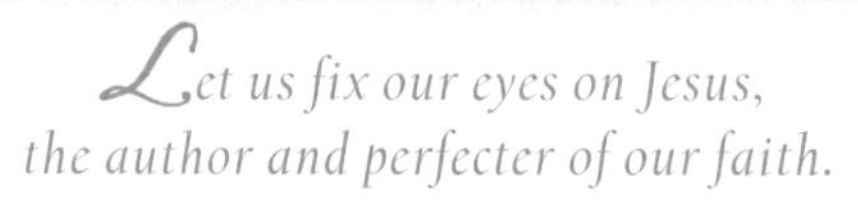

Date and Time: ____________________

Place: ____________________

Today, I was inspired by: ____________________

Other inspiring thoughts:

The sun. . .in its full glory, either at rising or setting—this, and many other like blessings we enjoy daily; and. . .because they are so common, most men forget to pay their praises. But let not us.

Izaak Walton

Everyone has a unique role to fill in the world and is important in some respect. Everyone, including and perhaps especially you, is indispensable.

NATHANIEL HAWTHORNE

Date and Time: __________

Place: __________

Today, I was inspired by: __________

Other inspiring thoughts:

Earth, with her thousand voices, praises God.

Samuel Taylor Coleridge

For GOD is sheer beauty, all-generous in love,
loyal always and ever.

PSALM 100:5 MSG

Date and Time: ______________________________

Place: ______________________________

Today, I was inspired by: ______________________________

Other inspiring thoughts:

Let us not hurry so in our pace of living that we lose sight of the art of living.

Sir Francis Bacon

Life is so full of meaning and purpose, so full of beauty beneath its covering, that you will find that earth but cloaks your heaven.

Fra Giovanni Giocondo

Date and Time: ______

Place: ______

Today, I was inspired by: ______

Other inspiring thoughts:

Being deeply loved by someone gives you strength, while loving someone deeply gives you courage.

LAO TZU

The steadfast love of the Lord never ceases, his mercies never come to an end; they are new every morning; great is your faithfulness.

LAMENTATIONS 3:22–23 NRSV

Date and Time: ______________________

Place: ______________________

Today, I was inspired by: ______________________

Other inspiring thoughts:

I would rather walk with God in the dark than go alone in the light.

Mary Brainard

In all ranks of life the human heart yearns for the beautiful; and the beautiful things that God makes are His gift to all alike.

HARRIET BEECHER STOWE

Date and Time: ____________________

Place: ____________________

Today, I was inspired by: ____________________

Other inspiring thoughts:

The riches that are in the heart cannot be stolen.

Russian Proverb

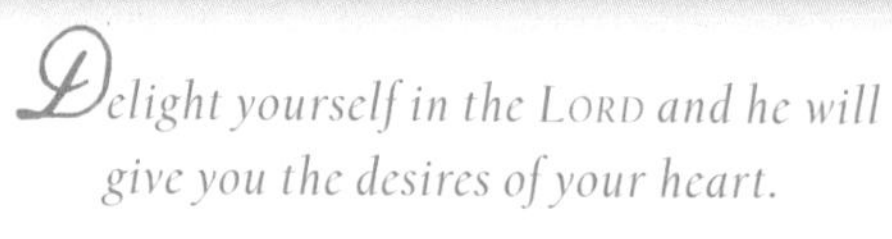

Date and Time: ______________________

Place: ______________________

Today, I was inspired by: ______________________

Other inspiring thoughts:

The world is charged with the grandeur of God.

Gerard Manley Hopkins

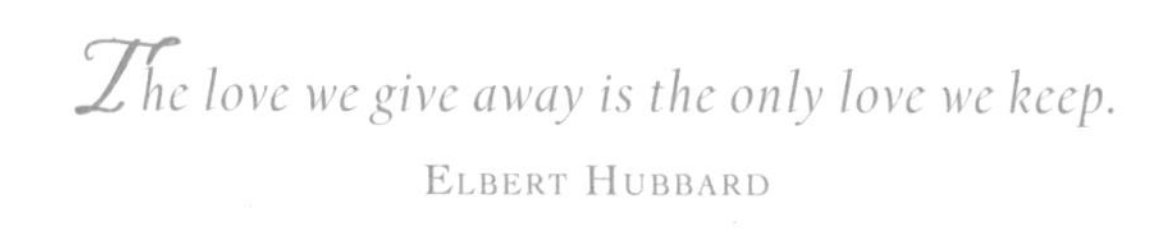

Date and Time:

Place:

Today, I was inspired by:

Other inspiring thoughts:

For in the true nature of things, if we will rightly consider, every green tree is far more glorious than if it were made of gold and silver.

MARTIN LUTHER

The LORD will guide you always; he will satisfy your needs in a sun-scorched land. . . . You will be like a well-watered garden, like a spring whose waters never fail.

ISAIAH 58:11 NIV

Date and Time: ____________________

Place: ____________________

Today, I was inspired by: ____________________

Other inspiring thoughts:

True silence is the rest of the mind; it is to the spirit what sleep is to the body, nourishment and refreshment.

William Penn

The longer I live, the more my mind dwells upon the beauty and the wonder of the world.

JOHN BURROUGHS

Date and Time: ______

Place: ______

Today, I was inspired by: ______

Other inspiring thoughts:

Every man's life is a fairy tale, written by God's fingers.

Hans Christian Andersen

Many, O LORD my God, are the wonders you have done. . . were I to speak and tell of them, they would be too many to declare.

PSALM 40:5 NIV

Date and Time: ______________________

Place: ______________________

Today, I was inspired by: ______________________

Other inspiring thoughts:

We are so preciously loved by God that we cannot even comprehend it. No created being can ever know how much and how sweetly and tenderly God loves them.

JULIAN OF NORWICH

All that is sweet, delightful, and amiable in this world. . .is nothing else but Heaven breaking through the veil of this world.

William Law

Date and Time:

Place:

Today, I was inspired by:

Other inspiring thoughts:

Happiness is a sunbeam. . . . When it strikes a kindred heart, like the converged lights upon a mirror, it reflects itself with redoubled brightness. It is not perfected until it is shared.

Jane Porter

The heavens declare the glory of God; the skies proclaim the work of his hands. Day after day they pour forth speech; night after night they display knowledge.

PSALM 19:1–2 NIV

Date and Time: ______________________

Place: ______________________

Today, I was inspired by: ______________________

Other inspiring thoughts:

God's gifts put man's best dreams to shame.

Elizabeth Barrett Browning

God writes the gospel not in the Bible alone,
but on trees and flowers and clouds and stars.

MARTIN LUTHER

Date and Time: __________

Place: __________

Today, I was inspired by: __________

Other inspiring thoughts:

Our Creator would never have made such lovely days, and have given us the deep hearts to enjoy them, above and beyond all thought, unless we were meant to be immortal.

Nathaniel Hawthorne

He counts the stars and assigns each a name.
Our Lord is great, with limitless strength;
we'll never comprehend what he knows and does.

PSALM 147:4–5 MSG

Date and Time:

Place:

Today, I was inspired by:

Other inspiring thoughts:

Be on the lookout for mercies.
The more we look for them, the more of them we will see.
Blessings brighten when we count them.

Maltbie D. Babcock

*Into all our lives, in many simple, familiar, homely ways,
God infuses this element of joy from the surprises of life,
which unexpectedly brighten our days, and fill our eyes with light.*

Henry Wadsworth Longfellow

Date and Time: __________

Place: __________

Today, I was inspired by: __________

Other inspiring thoughts:

What lies behind us and what lies before us are tiny matters compared to what lies within us.

Ralph Waldo Emerson

Now the God of hope fill you with all joy and peace in believing, that ye may abound in hope.

Romans 15:13 KJV

Date and Time: ______

Place: ______

Today, I was inspired by: ______

Other inspiring thoughts:

To me, every hour of the day and night is an unspeakably perfect miracle.

Walt Whitman

I avoid looking forward or backward,
and try to keep looking upward.

Charlotte Brontë

Date and Time: ______________________

Place: ______________________

Today, I was inspired by: ______________________

Other inspiring thoughts:

When the soul has laid down its faults at the feet of God, it feels as though it had wings.

Eugénie de Guérin

Your thoughts—how rare, how beautiful! God, I'll never comprehend them! I couldn't even begin to count them—any more than I could count the sand of the sea.

Psalm 139:17–18 MSG

Date and Time: ______

Place: ______

Today, I was inspired by: ______

Other inspiring thoughts:

Just as there comes a warm sunbeam into every cottage window, so comes a love—born of God's care for every separate need.

Nathaniel Hawthorne

Expect to have hope rekindled. Expect your prayers to be answered in wondrous ways. The dry seasons in life do not last. The spring rains will come again.

SARAH BAN BREATHNACH

Date and Time: ____________________

Place: ____________________

Today, I was inspired by: ____________________

Other inspiring thoughts:

Hope springs exulting on triumphant wing.

ROBERT BURNS

Open your mouth and taste,
open your eyes and see—how good God is.

Psalm 34:8 msg

Date and Time:

Place:

Today, I was inspired by:

Other inspiring thoughts:

This world, after all our science and sciences,
is still a miracle; wonderful, inscrutable, magical, and more.

THOMAS CARLYLE

Always be in a state of expectancy,
and see that you leave room for God to come in as He likes.

Oswald Chambers

Date and Time: ______

Place: ______

Today, I was inspired by: ______

Other inspiring thoughts:

Stars may be seen from the bottom of a deep well when they cannot be discerned from the top of a mountain.

Charles H. Spurgeon

My aim is to raise hopes by pointing the way to life without end. This is the life God promised long ago—and he doesn't break promises!

TITUS 1:2 MSG

Date and Time:

Place:

Today, I was inspired by:

Other inspiring thoughts:

Keep praying, but be thankful that God's answers are wiser than your prayers!

William Culbertson

It seems to me we can never give up longing and wishing while we are alive. There are certain things we feel to be beautiful and good, and we must hunger for them.

George Eliot

Date and Time: ____________________

Place: ____________________

Today, I was inspired by: ____________________

Other inspiring thoughts:

The private and personal blessings we enjoy. . .
. . .deserve the thanksgiving of a whole life.

Jeremy Taylor

"You'll go out in joy, you'll be led into a whole and complete life. The mountains and hills will lead the parade, bursting with song."

Isaiah 55:12 MSG

Date and Time: __________

Place: __________

Today, I was inspired by: __________

Other inspiring thoughts: ____________________

Live your life so that when you die others will know that you loved others clearly, loved your family dearly, and loved God completely.

Bruce Bickel and Stan Jantz

All our life is a celebration for us; we are convinced, in fact, that God is always everywhere.

Clement of Alexandria

Date and Time: ______

Place: ______

Today, I was inspired by: ______

Other inspiring thoughts:

In all things count on God—who does not change.

HOPE CLARKE

"If you have faith as small as a mustard seed, you can say to this mountain, 'Move from here to there' and it will move. Nothing will be impossible for you."

MATTHEW 17:20–21 NIV

Date and Time: ______

Place: ______

Today, I was inspired by: ______

Other inspiring thoughts:

True prayer is not to be found in the words of the mouth but in the thoughts of the heart.

Gregory the Great

*Only as high as I reach can I grow;
only as far as I seek can I go; only as deep as I look
can I see; only as much as I dream can I be.*

KAREN RAVN

Date and Time: __________

Place: __________

Today, I was inspired by: __________

Other inspiring thoughts:

God has amazing things in store for you.

Ellyn Sanna

Beloved, let us love one another: for love is of God; and every one that loveth is born of God, and knoweth God.

1 JOHN 4:7 KJV

Date and Time: ____________________

Place: ____________________

Today, I was inspired by: ____________________

Other inspiring thoughts:

Joy is not in things; it is in us.

Richard Wagner

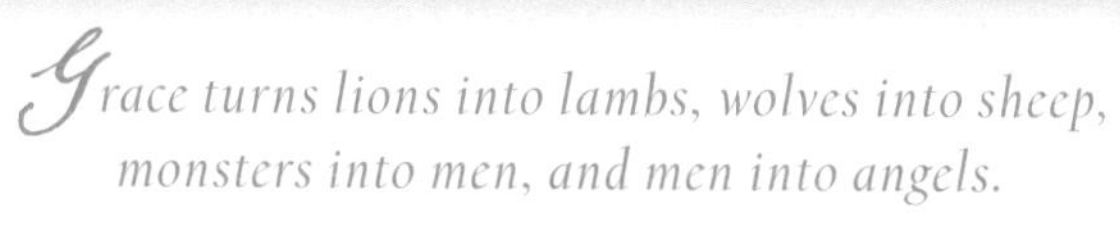

Grace turns lions into lambs, wolves into sheep, monsters into men, and men into angels.

Thomas Carlyle

Date and Time: ______________________

Place: ______________________

Today, I was inspired by: ______________________

Other inspiring thoughts:

Do not go where the path may lead,
go instead where there is no path and leave a trail.

Ralph Waldo Emerson

How great is the love the Father has lavished on us, that we should be called children of God! And that is what we are!

1 John 3:1 NIV

Date and Time: ____________________

Place: ____________________

Today, I was inspired by: ____________________

Other inspiring thoughts:

Simplicity is indeed often the sign of truth and a criterion of beauty.

Mahlon Hoagland

The patterns of our days are always changing. . .
rearranging. . .and each design for living is unique. . .
graced with its own special beauty.

Anonymous

Date and Time: ____

Place: ____

Today, I was inspired by: ____

Other inspiring thoughts:

Contentment is not the fulfillment of what you want,
but the realization of how much you already have.

Anonymous

Date and Time:

Place:

Today, I was inspired by:

Other inspiring thoughts:

The soul should always stand ajar,
ready to welcome the ecstatic experience.

Emily Dickinson

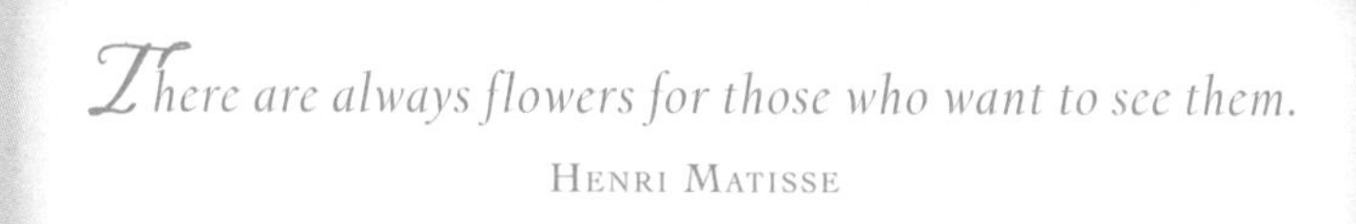

There are always flowers for those who want to see them.

HENRI MATISSE

Date and Time: ______________________________

Place: ______________________________

Today, I was inspired by: ______________________________

Other inspiring thoughts:

Always laugh when you can; it is cheap medicine. Merriment. . .is the sunny side of existence.

Lord Byron

But by the grace of God I am what I am.

1 Corinthians 15:10 KJV

Date and Time: ____________________

Place: ____________________

Today, I was inspired by: ____________________

Other inspiring thoughts:

There's surely something charming in seeing the smallest thing done so thoroughly, as if to remind the careless that whatever is worth doing is worth doing well.

Charles Dickens

An inexhaustible good nature is one of the most precious gifts of heaven.

Washington Irving

Date and Time: ______________________

Place: ______________________

Today, I was inspired by: ______________________

Other inspiring thoughts:

Life is like a mirror—
we get the best results when we smile at it.

Anonymous

May God be gracious to us and bless us
and make his face shine upon us.

PSALM 67:1 NIV

Date and Time: ____________________

Place: ____________________

Today, I was inspired by: ____________________

Other inspiring thoughts:

Do not forget little kindnesses and do not remember small faults.

Chinese Proverb

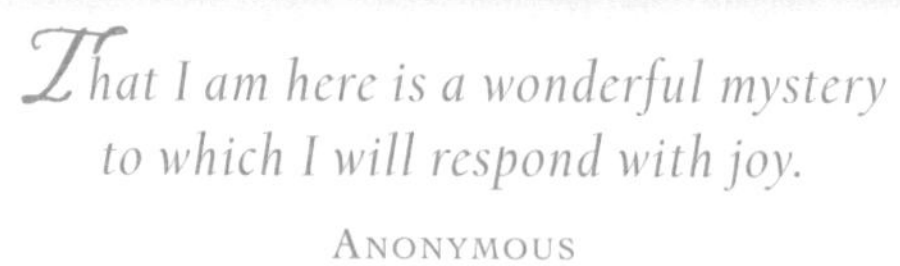

Date and Time: ______________________

Place: ______________________

Today, I was inspired by: ______________________

Other inspiring thoughts:

It's not what you look at that matters; it's what you see.

Henry David Thoreau

O Lord, be gracious to us; we long for you.
Be our strength every morning, our salvation in time of distress.

Isaiah 33:2 NIV

Date and Time: ______________________

Place: ______________________

Today, I was inspired by: ______________________

Other inspiring thoughts:

I asked God for all things that I might enjoy life.
He gave me life that I might enjoy all things.

Unknown

There's no substitute for plain, everyday goodness.

Maltbie D. Babcock

Date and Time: ______

Place: ______

Today, I was inspired by: ______

Other inspiring thoughts:

What we see depends mainly on what we look for.

John Lubbock

"The LORD bless you and keep you; the LORD make his face shine upon you and be gracious to you; the LORD turn his face toward you and give you peace."

NUMBERS 6:24–26 NIV

Date and Time: ____________________

Place: ____________________

Today, I was inspired by: ____________________

Other inspiring thoughts: ______________________________

____

____

____

____

____

____

____

____

____

____

____

____

____

____

____

____

____

____

Life is a flower of which love is the honey.

Victor Hugo

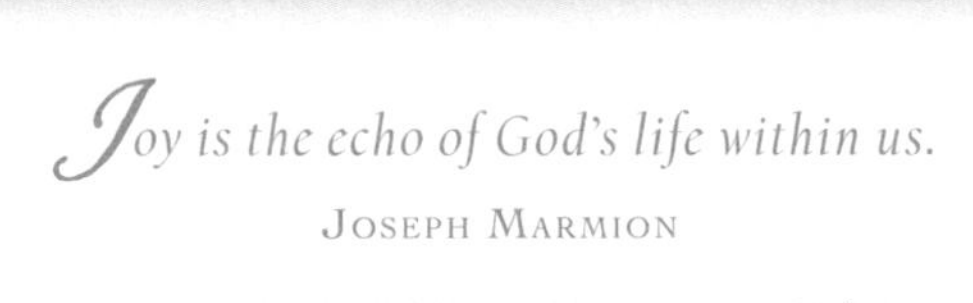

Date and Time: ______________________

Place: ______________________

Today, I was inspired by: ______________________

Other inspiring thoughts:

Every heart that has beat strong and cheerfully has left a hopeful impulse behind it in the world and bettered the tradition of mankind.

Robert Louis Stevenson

Take your everyday, ordinary life—your sleeping, eating, going-to-work, and walking-around life—and place it before God as an offering. Embracing what God does for you is the best thing you can do for him.

ROMANS 12:1 MSG

Date and Time: ____________________

Place: ____________________

Today, I was inspired by: ____________________

Other inspiring thoughts:

In all things of nature there is something of the marvelous.

Aristotle

Just living is not enough. . . .
One must have sunshine, freedom, and a little flower.

HANS CHRISTIAN ANDERSEN

Date and Time:

Place:

Today, I was inspired by:

Other inspiring thoughts:

Within each of us, just waiting to blossom,
is the wonderful promise of all we can be.

ANONYMOUS

I want you woven into a tapestry of love,
in touch with everything there is to know of God.

COLOSSIANS 2:2 MSG

Date and Time: ______________________

Place: ______________________

Today, I was inspired by: ______________________

Other inspiring thoughts:

Plant kindness and gather love.

ANONYMOUS

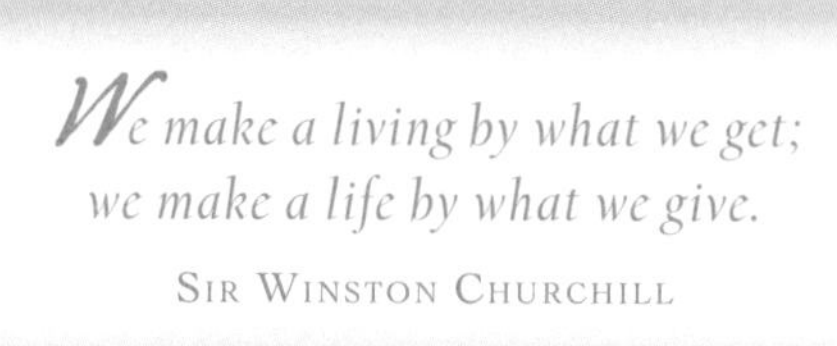

Date and Time: ____________________

Place: ____________________

Today, I was inspired by: ____________________

Other inspiring thoughts:

Though we travel the world over to find the beautiful, we must carry it with us or we find it not.

RALPH WALDO EMERSON

"Peace I leave with you; my peace I give you. I do not give to you as the world gives. Do not let your hearts be troubled and do not be afraid."

JOHN 14:27 NIV

Date and Time: ____________________

Place: ____________________

Today, I was inspired by: ____________________

Other inspiring thoughts:

We must take the moments of [God's] grace throughout the day with us: the music of the songbird in the morning, the kindness shown in the afternoon, and the restful sleep at night.

ANONYMOUS

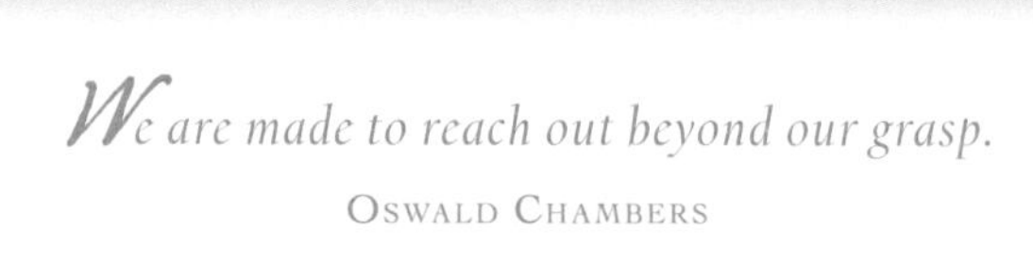

Date and Time: ______________________

Place: ______________________

Today, I was inspired by: ______________________

Other inspiring thoughts:

Love flies, runs, and rejoices;
it is free and nothing can hold it back.

Thomas à Kempis

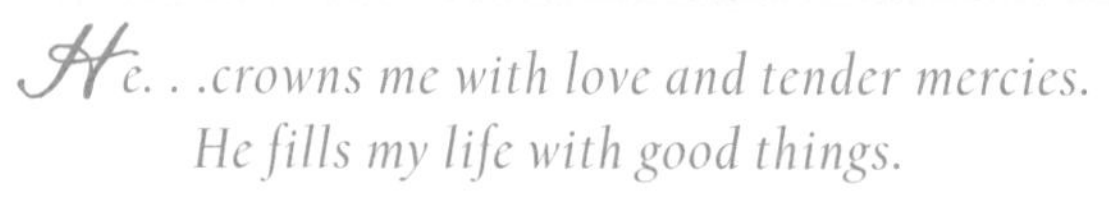

Psalm 103:4–5 NLT

Date and Time: ____________________

Place: ____________________

Today, I was inspired by: ____________________

Other inspiring thoughts: ______

Happiness cannot be traveled to, owned, earned, worn, or consumed. Happiness is the spiritual experience of living every minute with love, grace, and gratitude.

Denis Waitley

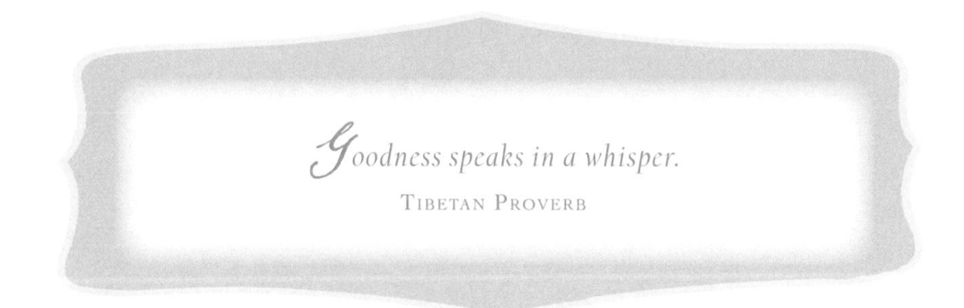

Date and Time:

Place:

Today, I was inspired by:

Other inspiring thoughts: ______________________________

I often think flowers are the angel's alphabet whereby they write on hills and fields mysterious and beautiful lessons for us to feel and learn.

LOUIS MAY ALCOTT

You have never seen [God] but you love Him. You cannot see Him now but you are putting your trust in Him. And you have joy so great that words cannot tell about it.

1 Peter 1:8 NLV

Date and Time: ______

Place: ______

Today, I was inspired by: ______

Other inspiring thoughts:

It isn't the great big pleasures that count the most; it's making a great deal out of the little ones.

Jean Webster

God loves us, and the will of love is always blessing for its loved ones.

HANNAH WHITALL SMITH

Date and Time: ____________________

Place: ____________________

Today, I was inspired by: ____________________

Other inspiring thoughts:

Let us acknowledge all good,
all delight that the world holds, and be content.

George MacDonald

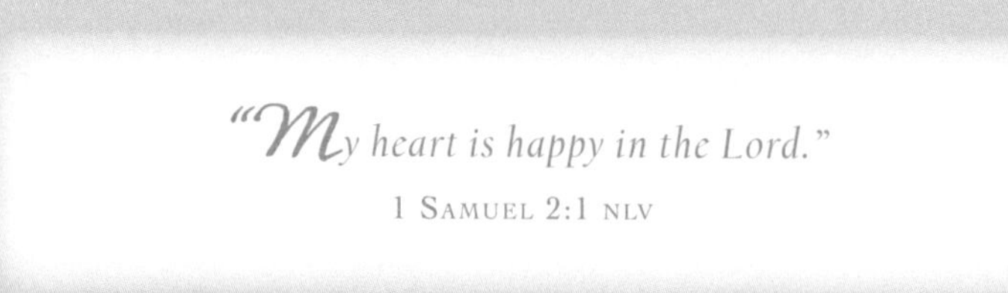

Date and Time:

Place:

Today, I was inspired by:

Other inspiring thoughts:

To be thankful for all is to accept grace to its fullest.

Anonymous

The Lord gives you the experience of enjoying His presence. He touches you, and His touch is so delightful that, more than ever, you are drawn inwardly to Him.

Jeanne Guyon

Date and Time: ______________________

Place: ______________________

Today, I was inspired by: ______________________

Other inspiring thoughts:

Nothing can separate you from His love, absolutely nothing. . . . God is enough for time, and God is enough for eternity. God is enough!

Hannah Whitall Smith

Surprise us with love at daybreak; then we'll skip and dance all the day long. . . . And let the loveliness of our Lord, our God, rest on us, confirming the work that we do.

PSALM 90:14, 17 MSG

Date and Time:

Place:

Today, I was inspired by:

Other inspiring thoughts:

All the world is an utterance of the Almighty. Its countless beauties, its exquisite adaptations, all speak to you of Him.

Phillips Brooks

And if tonight my soul may find her peace in sleep. . .
and in the morning wake like a new-opened flower,
then I have been dipped again in God, and new-created.

D. H. Lawrence

Date and Time:

Place:

Today, I was inspired by:

Other inspiring thoughts:

We may. . .depend upon God's promises, for. . .He will be as good as His word. He is so kind that He cannot deceive us, so true that He cannot break His promise.

Matthew Henry

For great is your love, higher than the heavens; your faithfulness reaches to the skies. Be exalted, O God, above the heavens, and let your glory be over all the earth.

PSALM 108:4–5 NIV

Date and Time: ____________________

Place: ____________________

Today, I was inspired by: ____________________

Other inspiring thoughts:

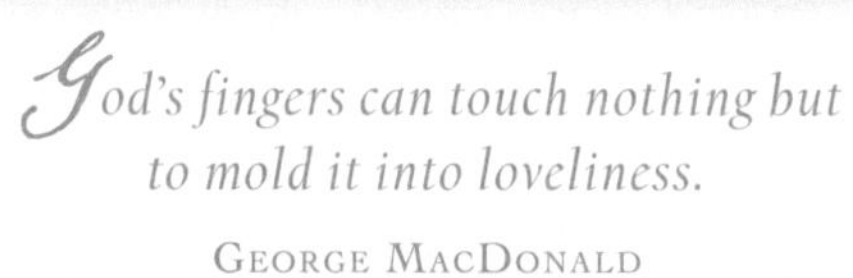

Our Lord does not care so much for the importance of our works as for the love with which they are done.

Teresa of Avila

Date and Time: ______

Place: ______

Today, I was inspired by: ______

Other inspiring thoughts:

When you have. . .accomplished your daily task, go to sleep in peace. God is awake.

Victor Hugo

But what happens when we live God's way? He brings gifts into our lives, much the same way that fruit appears in an orchard—things like affection for others, exuberance about life, serenity.

GALATIANS 5:22 MSG

Date and Time: ______________________

Place: ______________________

Today, I was inspired by: ______________________

Other inspiring thoughts:

The sun does not shine for a few trees and flowers,
but for the wide world's joy.

Henry Ward Beecher

If the day and the night are such that you greet them with joy, and life emits a fragrance like flowers and sweet-scented herbs, is more elastic, more starry, more immortal—that is your success.

Henry David Thoreau

Date and Time: ____________________

Place: ____________________

Today, I was inspired by: ____________________

Other inspiring thoughts:

*The more I study nature,
the more I am amazed at the Creator.*

Louis Pasteur

Steep yourself in God-reality, God-initiative, God-provisions. You'll find all your everyday human concerns will be met.

LUKE 12:30–31 MSG

Date and Time: ______

Place: ______

Today, I was inspired by: ______

Other inspiring thoughts:

God, who is love. . .simply cannot help but shed blessing on blessing upon us. We do not need to beg, for He simply cannot help it!

Hannah Whitall Smith

All I have seen teaches me to
trust the Creator for all I have not seen.

Ralph Waldo Emerson

Date and Time: ______________________

Place: ______________________

Today, I was inspired by: ______________________

Other inspiring thoughts:

This is and has been the Father's work from the beginning— to bring us into the home of His heart.

George MacDonald

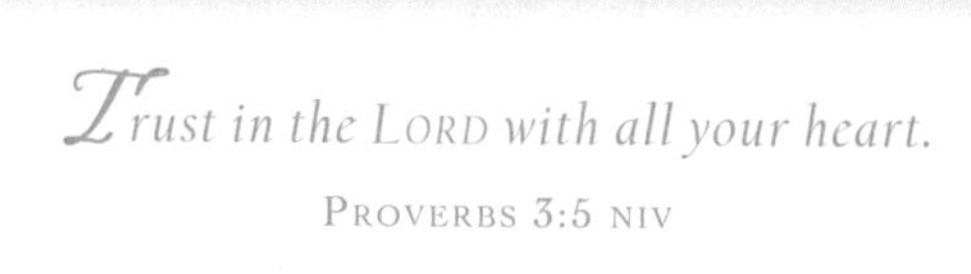

Date and Time: ______

Place: ______

Today, I was inspired by: ______

Other inspiring thoughts:

The greatest honor we can give God is to live gladly because of the knowledge of His love.

JULIAN OF NORWICH

How beautiful it is to be alive! To wake each morn as if the Maker's grace did us afresh from nothingness derive, that we might sing "How happy is our case! How beautiful it is to be alive!"

HENRY SEPTIMUS SUTTON

Date and Time: ______________________

Place: ______________________

Today, I was inspired by: ______________________

Other inspiring thoughts:

Seeing our Father in everything makes life one long thanksgiving and gives a rest of heart.

Hannah Whitall Smith

*"The LORD your God is with you, he is mighty to save.
He will take great delight in you, he will quiet you with his love,
he will rejoice over you with singing."*

ZEPHANIAH 3:17 NIV

Date and Time: __________

Place: __________

Today, I was inspired by: __________

Other inspiring thoughts:

Every day you shall wonder at yourself, at the richness of life which has come to you by the grace of God.

Phillips Brooks

Half the joy of life is in little things taken on the run. Let us run if we must. . .but let us keep our hearts young and our eyes open that nothing worth our while shall escape us.

Charles Victor Cherbuliez

Date and Time: __________

Place: __________

Today, I was inspired by: __________

Other inspiring thoughts:

The mere sense of living is joy enough.

Emily Dickinson

The LORD *pours down his blessings.*
Our land will yield its bountiful harvest.

PSALM 85:12 NLT

Date and Time: ______

Place: ______

Today, I was inspired by: ______

Other inspiring thoughts:

At some time in our life we feel a trembling, fearful longing to do some good thing. Life finds its noblest spring of excellence in this hidden impulse to do our best.

Robert Collyer

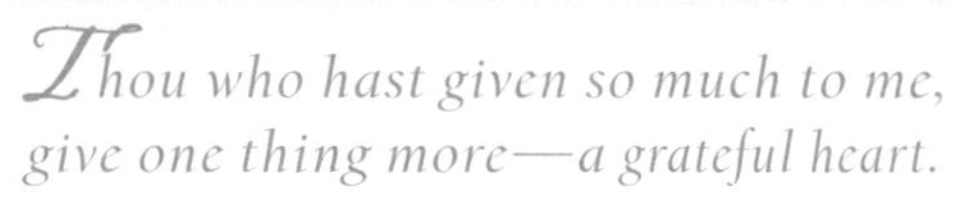

Thou who hast given so much to me,
give one thing more—a grateful heart.

George Herbert

Date and Time: ______

Place: ______

Today, I was inspired by: ______

Other inspiring thoughts:

Gratitude consists in a watchful, minute attention to the particulars of our state. . . . It fills us with a consciousness that God loves and cares for us, even to the least event and smallest need of life.

Henry Edward Manning

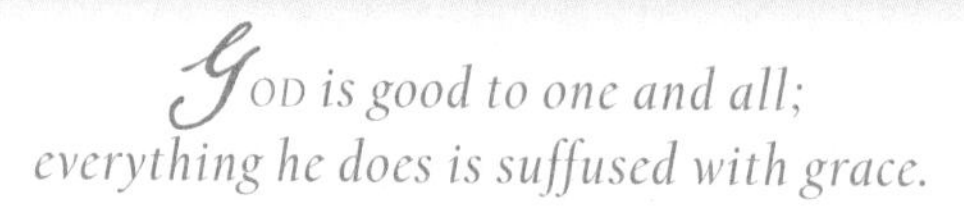

Date and Time:

Place:

Today, I was inspired by:

Other inspiring thoughts:

Optimism is the cheerful frame of mind that enables a teakettle to sing, though in hot water up to its nose.

Anonymous

Faith is the virtue by which, clinging to the faithfulness of God, we lean upon Him so that we may obtain what He gives us.

William Ames

Date and Time:

Place:

Today, I was inspired by:

Other inspiring thoughts:

There is nothing that makes us love a man so much as praying for him.

WILLIAM LAW

Date and Time: ____________________

Place: ____________________

Today, I was inspired by: ____________________

Other inspiring thoughts:

We do not need to search. . .to find our eternal Father. In fact, we do not even need to speak out loud, for though we speak in the smallest whisper or the most fleeting thought, He is close enough to hear us.

Teresa of Avila

In prayer it is better to have a heart without words than words without a heart.

JOHN BUNYAN

Date and Time: ______

Place: ______

Today, I was inspired by: ______

Other inspiring thoughts:

Angels fly because they take themselves lightly.

UNKNOWN

Date and Time: ________________________________

Place: ______________________________________

Today, I was inspired by: ________________________

Other inspiring thoughts:

A keen sense of humor helps us to overlook the unbecoming,
understand the unconventional, tolerate the unpleasant,
overcome the unexpected, and outlast the unbearable.

Billy Graham

Date and Time: ____________________

Place: ____________________

Today, I was inspired by: ____________________

Other inspiring thoughts:

When the solution is simple, God is answering.

Albert Einstein

Trust should be in God,
who richly gives us all we need for our enjoyment.

1 Timothy 6:17 NLT

Date and Time: ______

Place: ______

Today, I was inspired by: ______

Other inspiring thoughts:

Carve your name on hearts and not on marble.

CHARLES SPURGEON

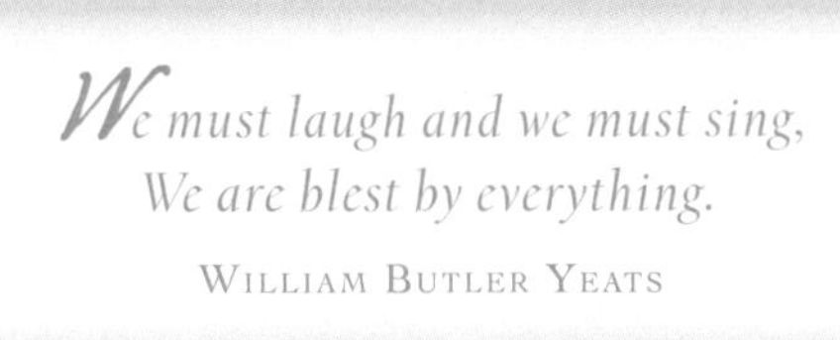

We must laugh and we must sing,
We are blest by everything.

WILLIAM BUTLER YEATS

Date and Time: ______________________________

Place: ______________________________

Today, I was inspired by: ______________________________

Other inspiring thoughts:

It is astonishing how short a time it takes
for very wonderful things to happen.

Frances Hodgson Burnett

You have made known to me the path of life;
you will fill me with joy in your presence,
with eternal pleasures at your right hand.

PSALM 16:11 NIV

Date and Time: ______

Place: ______

Today, I was inspired by: ______

Other inspiring thoughts:

Big doesn't necessarily mean better. Sunflowers aren't better than violets.

Edna Ferber

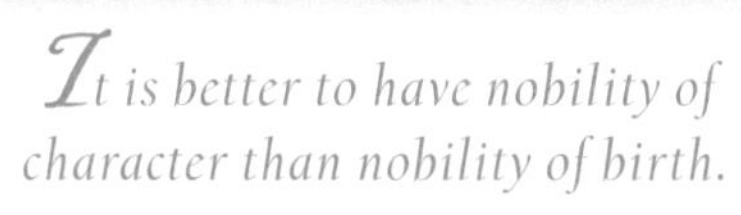

It is better to have nobility of character than nobility of birth.

Jewish Proverb

Date and Time: ____________________

Place: ____________________

Today, I was inspired by: ____________________

Other inspiring thoughts:

Joy is very infectious; therefore, be always full of joy.

Mother Teresa

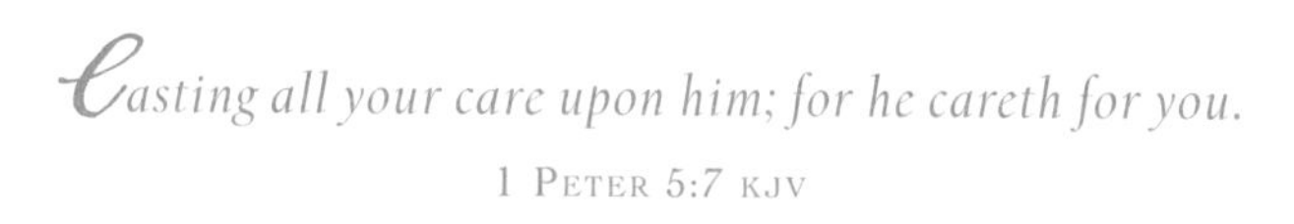

Date and Time: ____________________

Place: ____________________

Today, I was inspired by: ____________________

Other inspiring thoughts:

Nothing contributes more to cheerfulness than the habit of looking at the good side of things.

William B. Ullathorne

By reading the scriptures I am so renewed that all nature seems renewed around me and with me. . . . The whole world is charged with the glory of God, and I feel fire and music under my feet.

THOMAS MERTON

Date and Time: ____________________

Place: ____________________

Today, I was inspired by: ____________________

Other inspiring thoughts:

And life is what we make it.
Always has been, always will be.

Grandma Moses

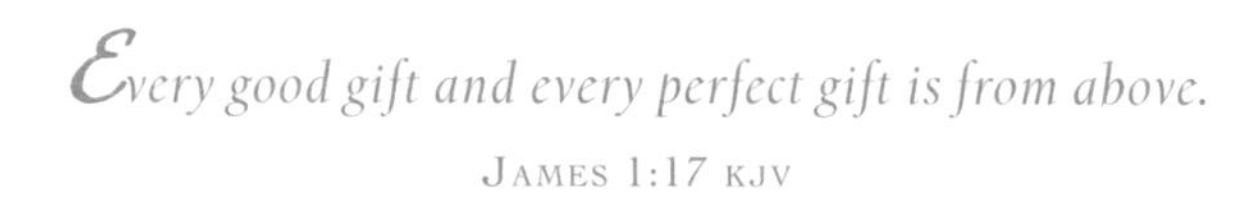

Every good gift and every perfect gift is from above.

James 1:17 KJV

Date and Time: ______________________

Place: ______________________

Today, I was inspired by: ______________________